MISSAL

BILINGUAL TEXT
(LATIN-ENGLISH)
OF THE ORDER OF MASS
IN THE EXTRAORDINARY FORM

Selection, design and composition:
Fr. Enrique Escribano
English translation (notes):
Fr. James Kotch
Fr. Enrique Escribano

First edition
Guayaquil, Ecuador, July 15th, 2022
Version 1.00

Shoreless Lake Press

Keys to follow the Holy Mass

<u>In double column text:</u>

In the center: Explanations: in small print and in red.

In the left column: The Holy Mass in Latin.

- **Words to say: in blue.**

- Words that the priest says: in black.

In the right column: English translation.

<u>In the margins:</u>

Postures, gestures and sounds:

On the left what you do:

Standing

Sitting

On knees

Genuflection

Walk

Tapping chest

Crossing yourself (from forehead to chest)

Crossing your forehead, lips and heart

On the right what others do:

Priest puts his hand on the altar

Priest kisses the book

Priest in a loud voice

Priest in a middle voice

Priest in a low voice

Bell sound

Within the text:

Priest makes some cross

THE ORDER OF MASS

Holy Mass is divided into two main parts: the Mass of the Catechumens, preparatory for the Holy Sacrifice, and the Mass of the Faithful, which is properly the Holy Sacrifice.

FIRST PART
MASS OF THE CATECHUMENS

The Mass of the Catechumens runs from the beginning to the Offertory. In it, the Holy Sacrifice is prepared by means of:
a) Prayer: The prayers at the foot of the altar, Kyrie and other prayers.
b) Praise: Introit, Gloria, Gradual and Hallelujah.
c) Instruction: Epistle, Gospel, Sermon and Creed.

1. - Preparatory and prayers at the foot of the altar

Holy Mass begins with the entrance procession. Once the Celebrant reaches the altar, prepares the Chalice and has opened the Missal, descends the steps, genuflects to the Blessed Sacrament enclosed in the Tabernacle and begins with the sign of the Cross.

In nómine Patris et Fílii † et Spíritus Sancti. Amen.

In the name of the Father, † and of the Son, and of the Holy Spirit. Amen.

Introíbo ad altáre Dei.

I will go to the altar of God.

Ad Deum qui lætíficat iuventútem meam.

To God who gives joy to my youth.

Psalm 42

This psalm is omitted in the Masses for the dead and in the time of passion, jumping to the *Adiutorium*, on page 6

Júdica me, Deus, et discérne causam meam de gente non sancta: ab hómine iníquo, et dolóso érue me.

Judge me, 0 God, and defend my cause against an unholy nation; from the unjust and deceitful deliver me.

Quia tu es, Deus, fortitúdo mea: quare me repulísti et quare tristis incédo dum afflígit me inimícus?

For thou art my God and my strength: why dost thou reject me? Why should I go away in sadness, oppressed by the enemy?

Emítte lucem tuam, et veritátem tuam: ipsa me deduxérunt, et adduxérunt in montem sanctum tuum, et in tabernácula tua.

Send forth thy light and thy truth; may they guide and lead me to thy holy hill, to the place where thou dwellest.

Et introíbo ad altáre Dei: ad Deum qui lætíficat iuventútem meam.

I shall go to the altar of God, to God who gives me youthful joy.

Confitébor tibi in cíthara, Deus, Deus meus: quare tristis es ánima mea, et quare contúrbas me?

I shall praise thee on the harp, 0 God, my God; why art thou downcast, my soul, why art thou in a turmoil within me?

Spera in Deo, quóniam adhuc confitébor illi: salutáre vultus mei, et Deus meus.	Hope in God: I shall praise him again, my Saviour and my God.
Glória Patri, et Fílio, et Spirítui Sancto.	Glory be to the Father, and to the Son, and to the Holy Spirit.
Sicut erat in princípio, et nunc, et semper; et in sǽcula sæculórum. Amen.	As it was in the beginning, is now and ever shall be, world without end. Amen.
Introíbo ad altáre Dei	I will go to the altar of God.
Ad Deum qui lætíficat iuventútem meam.	To God who gives me youthful joy.

Prayed Psalm 42 is continued

Adiutórium † nostrum in nómine Dómini.	Our † help is in the name of the Lord.
Qui fecit cælum et terram.	Who made heaven and earth.

Act of Contrition

To draw near to God we must first humble ourselves and publicly acknowledge ourselves as sinners. The priest prays "I confess" first and then the assembly prays it. Then we receive from the Celebrant the absolution of venial sins

Confíteor Deo omnipoténti, beátæ Maríæ semper Vírgini, beáto Michǽli Archángelo, beáto Ioanni Baptístæ, sanctis Apóstolis Petro et Paulo, ómnibus Sanctis, et vobis, fratres: quia peccávi nimis cogitatióne, verbo et ópere: mea culpa, mea culpa, mea máxima culpa. Ideo precor beátam Maríam semper Vírginem, beátum Michǽlem Archángelum, beátum Ioánnem Baptístam, sanctos Apóstolos Petrum et Paulum, omnes Sanctos, et vos, fratres, oráre pro me ad Dóminum Deum nostrum.

I confess to almighty God, to blessed Mary ever Virgin, to blessed Michael the Archangel, to blessed John the Baptist, to the holy Apostles Peter and Paul, to all the Saints and to you, brethren, that I have sinned exceedingly in thought, word, and deed: through my fault, through my fault, through my most grievous fault. Therefore I beseech the blessed Mary ever Virgin, blessed Michael the Archangel, blessed John the Baptist, the holy apostles Peter and Paul, all the Saints and you, brethren, to pray to the Lord our God for me.

Misereátur tui omnípotens Deus, et dimíssis peccátis tuis, perdúcat te ad vitam ætérnam.

May almighty God have mercy on you, forgive your sins and bring you to everlasting life.

Amen.

Amen.

Confíteor Deo omnipoténti, beátæ Maríæ semper Vírgini, beáto Michǽli Archángelo, beáto Ioanni Baptístæ, sanctis Apóstolis Petro et Paulo, ómnibus Sanctis, et tibi, Pater; quia peccávi nimis cogitatióne, verbo et ópere, mea CULPA, mea CULPA, mea máxima CULPA. Ideo precor beátam Maríam semper Vírginem, beátum Michǽlem Archángelum, beátum Ioánnem Baptístam, sanctos Apóstolos Petrum et Paulum, omnes Sanctos, et te, Pater, oráre pro me ad Dóminum Deum nostrum.

I confess to almighty God, to blessed Mary ever Virgin, to blessed Michael the Archangel, to blessed John the Baptist, to the holy Apostles Peter and Paul, to all the Saints and to you, Father, that I have sinned exceedingly in thought, word, and deed: through my fault, through my fault, through my most grievous fault. Therefore I beseech the blessed Mary ever Virgin, blessed Michael the Archangel, blessed John the Baptist, the holy apostles Peter and Paul, all the Saints and you, Father, to pray to the Lord our God for me.

Misereátur vestri omnípotens Deus, et dimíssis pecátis vestris, perdúcat vos ad vitam ætérnam.

May almighty God be merciful to you, forgive your sins and bring you to everlasting life.

Amen.

Amen.

✝ **I**ndulgéntiam, † absolutiónem et remissiónem peccatórum nostrórum, tríbuat nobis omnípotens et miséricors Dóminus.

May the almighty and merciful Lord grant us pardon, † absolution and remission of our sins.

Amen.

Amen.

Deus, tu convérsus vivificábis nos.

Turn to us, 0 God, and give us life.

Et plebs tua lætábitur in te.

And thy people will find joy in thee.

Osténde nobis, Dómine, misericórdiam tuam.

Show us, Lord, thy mercy.

Et salutáre tuum da nobis.

And give us thy salvation.

Dómine, exáudi oratiónem meam.

Lord, hear my prayer.

Et clamor meus ad te véniat.

And let my cry reach thee.

Dóminus vobíscum.

The Lord be with you.

Et cum spíritu tuo.

And with your spirit.

Orémus.

Let us pray.

The priest goes up to the altar while praying in a low voice

Aufer a nobis, quǽsumus, Dómine, iniquitátes nostras: ut ad Sancta sanctórum puris mereámur méntibus introíre. Per Christum Dóminum nostrum. Amen.

Take from us our sins, we beg thee, Lord; that we may enter the holy of holies with pure minds. Through Christ our Lord. Amen

Orámus te, Dómine, per mérita Sanctórum tuórum, quorum relíquiæ hic sunt,…

We pray thee, Lord, through the merits of thy Saints, whose relics are here,…

The priest kisses the altar with the relics of the holy martyrs

…et ómnium Sanctórum: ut indulgére dignéris ómnia peccáta mea. Amen.

…and of all the Saints, to pardon all my sins. Amen.

In some Masses incense is used at this time

2. - Introit

This is the first proper prayer of the Mass for the day, which you will not find in this missal because it is different every day. If the choir sings the Kyrie, the priest says the introit in a low voice. The priest says the entire prayer and then repeats the first part

3. - Kyrie and Gloria

The priest goes to the center of the altar
If the choir sings the Kyrie the priest prays the Kyrie in a low voice

 **K**ýrie, eléison   **L**ord, have mercy

Kýrie, eléison   Lord, have mercy

Kýrie, eléison   Lord, have mercy

Christe, eléison   Christ, have mercy

Christe, eléison   Christ, have mercy

Christe, eléison   Christ, have mercy

Kýrie, eléison   Lord, have mercy

Kýrie, eléison   Lord, have mercy

Kýrie, eléison   Lord, have mercy

The assembly does not pray the Gloria but they do sing it.
It is omitted in Masses with purple vestments, or with
green during the week and in votive Masses

Glória in excelsis Deo; et in terra pax homínibus bonæ voluntátis. Laudámus te. Benedícimus te. Adorámus te. Glorificámus te. Grátias ágimus tibi propter mag-

Glory to God in the highest, and on earth peace to men of good will. We praise thee, we bless thee, we adore thee, we glorify thee, we give thanks to thee for thy great glory, Lord God, heavenly

- 11 -

nam glóriam tuam. Dómine Deus, Rex cæléstis, Deus Pater omnípotens. Dómine Fili Unigénite, Iesu Christe. Dómine Deus, Agnus Dei, Fílius Patris. Qui tollis peccáta mundi, miserére nobis. Qui tollis peccáta mundi, súscipe deprecatiónem nostram. Qui sedes ad déxteram Patris, miserére nobis. Quóniam tu solus Sanctus. Tu solus Dóminus. Tu solus Altíssimus, Iesu Christe. Cum Sancto Spíritu in glória ✝ Dei Patris. Amen.

King, God the Father almighty. Lord Jesus Christ the only-begotten Son, Lord God, Lamb of God, Son of the Father, who takest away the sins of the world, have mercy on us; who takest away the sins of the world, receive our prayer; who sittest at the right hand of the Father, have mercy on us. For thou alone art holy, thou alone art Lord, thou alone art the most high: Jesus Christ with the Holy Spirit, in the glory ✝ of God the Father. Amen.

The priest greets the people saying:

Dóminus vobíscum.

The Lord be with you.

Et cum spíritu tuo.

And with your spirit.

4. - Collect Prayer

Orémus.

Let us pray.

The second proper prayer of the Mass for the day is said. There may be several "Collect" prayers, depending on the rite and category of the celebration. The end of the first and last (if there are several) prayer ends as follows, answering: Amen

...per ómnia sæcula sæculórum.

...for ever and ever.

Amen.

Amen.

5. - First Biblical Reading: The Epistle

Every day is different. After the epistle, the priest places his left hand touching the altar or simply raises it as a sign that the reading has finished and those present answer:

Deo grátias.   Thanks be to God.

6. - Psalmody: Gradual, Alleluia and Tract

Proper prayer of the Mass for each day.
In Lent the Tract is prayed instead of the Alleluia

7. - Second Biblical Reading: The Gospel

Before beginning, the priest prays bowed in the center of the altar:

Munda cor meum ac lábia mea, omnípotens Deus, qui lábia Isaíæ Prophétæ cálculo mundásti igníto: ita me tua grata miseratióne dignáre mundáre, ut sanctum Evangélium tuum digne váleam nuntiáre. Per Christum Dóminum nostrum. Amen.
Iube, Dómine, benedícere.
Dóminus sit in corde meo et in lábiis meis, ut digne et competénter annúntiem evangélium suum. Amen.

Cleanse my heart and my lips, almighty God, who didst cleanse the lips of the prophet Isaias with a glowing coal: in thy gracious mercy be pleased so to cleanse me, that I may worthily proclaim thy holy Gospel. Through Christ our Lord. Amen.
Pray, Lord, a blessing.

May the Lord be in my heart and on my lips that I may announce his Gospel worthily and well. Amen.

The Gospel is prayed on the left side of the altar

Dóminus vobíscum. The Lord be with you.

Et cum spíritu tuo. And with your spirit.

equéntia sancti † Evangélii † secúndum † *"N"*.

passage from † the holy Gospel † according to † *"N"*.

Where "N" is the name of the evangelist whose Gospel is to be read

Glória tibi, Dómine. Glory to thee, 0 Lord.

After the Gospel is finished, the priest kisses the book and responds:

Laus tibi, Christe. Praise to thee, 0 Christ.

After kissing the Gospel the priest says in secret:

Per evangélica dicta, deleántur nostra delícta.

Through the words of the Gospel may our sins be forgiven.

Sermon

If there happens to be one

8. - Creed
It is only prayed on Sundays and on Holy Days of Obligation, or special Feasts of Our Lord, the Blessed Virgin, the Apostles, etc...

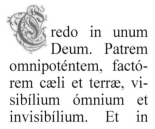redo in unum Deum. Patrem omnipoténtem, factórem cæli et terræ, visibílium ómnium et invisibílium. Et in

believe in one God, the almighty Father, maker of heaven and earth, and of all things visible and invisible. I believe in one Lord Jesus Christ, on-

unum Dóminum Iesum Christum, Fílium Dei Unigénitum. Et ex Patre natum ante ómnia sǽcula. Deum de Deo, lumen de lúmine, Deum verum de Deo vero. Génitum, non factum, consubstantiálem Patri: per quem ómnia facta sunt. Qui propter nos hómines, et propter nostram salútem descéndit de cælis.

ET INCARNÁTUS EST DE SPÍRITU SANCTO EX MARÍA VÍRGINE: ET HOMO FACTUS EST.

Crucifíxus etiam pro nobis: sub Póntio Pilato passus, et sepúltus est. Et resurréxit tértia die, secúndum Scriptúras. Et ascéndit in cælum: sedet ad déxteram Patris. Et íterum ventúrus est cum glória iudicáre vivos et mórtuos: cuius regni non erit finis. Et in Spíritum Sanctum, Dóminum et vivificántem: qui ex Patre Filióque procédit. Qui cum Patre, et Filio simul adorátur et conglorificátur: qui locútus est per

ly-begotten Son of God, born of the Father before all ages ; God from God, light from light, true God from true God, begotten not made, one in substance with the Father: through whom all things were made. For us men and for our salvation, he came down from heaven,

WAS INCARNATE OF BY THE HOLY SPIRIT FROM THE VIRGIN MARY, AND WAS MADE MAN.

He was also crucified for us, suffered under Pontius Pilate and was buried. On the third day he rose again, according to the Scriptures. He ascended into heaven, and sits at the right hand of the Father. He will come again in glory to judge the living and the dead; and his reign will have no end. I believe also in the Holy Spirit, Lord and giver of life, who proceeds from the Father and the Son; who together with the Father and the Son is adored and

Prophétas. Et unam, sanctam, catholicam et Apostólicam Ecclésiam. Confíteor unum baptísma in remissiónem peccatórum. Et exspécto resurrectiónem mortuórum. Et vitam ventúri † sǽculi. Amen.

glorified; who spoke through the Prophets. And I believe in one, holy, catholic and apostolic Church. I confess one baptism for the remission of sins. And I look for the resurrection of the dead, and the life of the world † that is to come. Amen.

SECOND PART
MASS OF THE FAITHFUL

This is the actual Sacrifice, and contains:

a) Offertory: The blessing or separation of the matter;

b) Consecration: The oblation of the Victim;

c) Communion: Participation in the Sacrifice.

Jesus Christ on the eve of his Passion (here I have mentioned the Sacrifice of the Mass, which is the same as Calvary), took bread in his holy and venerable hands (here is the blessing or separation of matter) ... and gave thanks to God blessed him (here is the offering of the Victim), he broke it and gave it to his disciples (here is the communion or participation).

a) THE OFFERTORY

The priest greets the people saying:

Dóminus vobíscum.

The Lord be with you.

Et cum spíritu tuo.

And with you also.

9. - Offertory prayer

Orémus:

Let us pray.

Here follows a prayer of the day

10. - Offering of the Host

Súscipe, sancte Pater, omnípotens ætérne Deus, hanc immaculátam hóstiam, quam ego indígnus fámulus tuus óffero tibi, Deo meo vivo et vero, pro innumerabílibus peccátis, et offensiónibus, et negligéntiis meis, et pro ómnibus circumstántibus, sed et pro ómnibus fidélibus Christiánis vivis atque defúnctis: ut mihi, et illis profíciat ad salútem in vitam ætérnam. Amen.

Holy Father, almighty eternal God, receive the sacrifice of this perfect offering, which I thy unworthy servant make to thee, my living and true God, for my sins and offences and negligences without number, and for all who are present here as well as for all the Christian faithful living and dead: that it may prosper their salvation and mine unto life everlasting. Amen.

11. - Offering of the Chalice

The water is blessed in the preparation of the chalice

Deus, † qui humánæ substántiæ dignitátem mirabíliter condidísti, et mirabílius reformásti: da nobis per húius aquæ et vini mystérium, eius divinitátis esse consórtes, qui humanitátis nostræ fíeri dignátus est párticeps, Iesus Christus Fílius tuus Dóminus noster: Qui tecum vivit et regnat in

God, † who in a wonderful manner hast formed the noble nature of man and even more wonderfully reformed it, grant that by the mystery of this water and wine, we may have fellowship in his Godhead, who deigned to share our manhood, Jesus Christ thy Son our Lord, who liveth and reigneth with thee in the unity of

unitáte Spíritus Sancti Deus: per ómnia sǽcula sæculórum. Amen.

the Holy Spirit, God, for ever and ever. Amen.

At the end of which, the chalice is offered up

fférimus tibi, Dómine, cálicem salutáris, tuam deprecántes cleméntiam: ut in conspéctu divínæ maiestátis tuæ, pro nostra et totíus mundi salúte, cum odóre suavitátis ascéndat. Amen.

e offer thee, 0 Lord, the chalice of salvation, beseeching thy gentle mercy, that for our own and the whole world's salvation it may ascend with a sweet fragrance in the sight of thy divine majesty. Amen.

12. - Offering of the Priest and the faithful
We ask to be a pleasant offering despite our unworthiness

n spíritu humilitátis et in ánimo contríto suscipiámur a te, Dómine: et sic fiat sacrifícium nostrum in conspéctu tuo hódie, ut pláceat tibi, Dómine Deus.

ith humble soul and repentant heart may we be received by thee, Lord; and may our sacrifice be so offered in thy sight this day that it may please thee, Lord God.

Offerings are blessed

eni, sanctificátor omnípotens ætérne Deus: et béne†dic hoc sacrifícium, tuo sancto nómini præparátum.

ome Sanctifier, almighty eternal God, and † bless this sacrifice, prepared for thy holy name.

At some Masses, incense is used here. The members of the assembly stand to be incensed; then they take their seats again.

13. - Washing of the hands
Psalm 25

avábo inter innocéntes manus meas: et circúmdabo altáre tuum, Dómine.

Ut áudiam vocem laudis: et enárrem univérsa mirabília tua.

Dómine, diléxi decórem domus tuæ: et locum habitatiónis glóriæ tuæ.

Ne perdas cum ímpiis, Deus, ánimam meam: et cum viris sánguinum vitam meam.

In quorum mánibus iniquitátes sunt: déxtera eórum repléta est munéribus.

Ego autem in innocéntia mea ingréssus sum: rédime me, et miserére mei.

Pes meus stetit in dirécto: in ecclésiis benedícam te, Dómine.

Glória Patri, et Fílio, et Spirítui Sancto.

Sicut erat in princípio, et nunc, et semper: et in sǽcula sæculórum. Amen.

I will wash my hands among the innocent and gather with them at thy altar, Lord.

To hear the song of praise and tell of all thy wonderful works.

Lord, I have loved the beauty of thy house and the place where thy glory dwells.

Let not my soul, 0 God, be lost among the wicked nor my life with men of blood.

Their hands are steeped in evil; their right hands full of bribes.

For myself, I walk in innocence; redeem me and be merciful to me.

My feet are set in the straight path: where men gather, Lord, I will bless thee.

Glory be to the Father, and to the Son, and to the Holy Spirit.

As it was in the beginning, is now, and ever shall be: world without end. Amen.

14. - Invocation

Returning to the middle of the altar and bowed, the Priest offers to the Holy Trinity the Sacrifice he is celebrating, asking for intercession saying:

úscipe, sancta Trínitas, hanc oblatiónem, quam tibi offérimus ob memóriam passiónis, resurrectiónis, et ascensiónis Iesu Christi, Dómini nostri: et in honórem beátæ Maríæ semper Vírginis, et beáti Ioánnis Baptístæ, et sanctórum Apostolórum Petri et Páuli, et istórum, et ómnium sanctórum: ut illis profíciat ad honórem, nobis autem ad salútem: et illi pro nobis intercédere dignéntur in cælis, quorum memóriam ágimus in terris. Per eúndem Christum Dóminum nostrum. Amen.

eceive, 0 holy Trinity, this offering which we make to thee in memory of the passion, resurrection and ascension of Jesus Christ our Lord, and in honour of the blessed Mary ever Virgin, of blessed John the Baptist, of the holy Apostles Peter and Paul, of those whose relics are here, and of all the Saints; that it may bring honour to them and salvation to us; and may they, whose memory we keep on earth, be pleased to intercede for us in heaven: through the same Christ our Lord. Amen.

15. - Exchange of prayers

The Priest kisses the altar, turns to the people and, opening and closing his arms as if to embrace everyone in the name of Christ, whose place he is taking, commends himself to their prayers saying:

 ráte, fratres:...

ray, brethren,...

...ut meum ac vestrum sa-

...that my sacrifice and

- 20 -

crifícium acceptábile fiat apud Deum Patrem... ...omnipoténtem.

yours may find acceptance with God the Father… …almighty.

Suscípiat Dóminus sacrifícium de mánibus tuis ad láudem et glóriam nóminis sui, ad utilitátem quoque nostram, totiúsque Ecclésiæ suæ sanctæ.

May the Lord receive the sacrifice from your hands for the praise and glory of his name, for our welfare also, and that of all his holy Church.

Amen.

Amen.

16. - Secret Prayer

Proper prayer for each day. They can be several. It ends with the Preface

b) THE CONSECRATION
17. - Preface

...per ómnia sǽcula sæculórum.

...for ever and ever.

Amen.

Amen.

Dóminus vobíscum.

The Lord be with you.

Et cum spíritu tuo.

And with your spirit.

Sursum corda.

Raise your hearts.

Habémus ad Dóminum.

They are raised to the Lord.

Gratias agámus Dómino Deo nostro.

Let us give thanks to the Lord our God.

Dignum et iustum est.

It is just and right.

Preface

The following Preface is the most common Sunday Preface, but there are different Prefaces for Easter, Christmas, Lent, some Holy Days...

ere dignum et iustum est, æquum et salutáre, nos tibi semper, et ubíque grátias ágere: Dómine sancte, Pater omnípotens, ætérne Deus. Qui cum unigénito Fílio tuo, et Spíritu Sancto, unus es Deus, unus es Dóminus: non in uníus singularitáte persónæ, sed in uníus Trinitáte substántiæ. Quod enim de tua glória, revelánte te, crédimus, hoc de Fílio tuo, hoc de Spíritu Sancto, sine differéntia discretiónis sentímus. Ut in confessióne veræ, sempiternæque Deitátis, et in persónis propríetas, et in esséntia únitas, et in maiestáte adorétur æquálitas. Quam laudant Ángeli atque Archángeli, Chérubim quoque ac Séraphim: qui non cessant clamáre quotídie, una voce dicéntes:

t is truly just and right, fitting and for our good, always and everywhere to give thanks to thee, Lord, holy Father, almighty eternal God; who with thine only-begotten Son and the Holy Spirit art one God, one Lord, not in the singleness of one person but in the one substance of the Trinity. For whatever through thy revelation we believe concerning thy glory, that also we hold both of thy Son and of the Holy Spirit, without distinction or difference; so that in confessing the true and everlasting Godhead, we adore each several person, and at the same time their one substance and their equal majesty; which the Angels praise and the Archangels, the Cherubim too and Seraphim, who never cease to cry out every day, saying with one voice:

Sanctus, Sanctus, Sanctus Dóminus Deus Sábaoth. Pleni sunt cæli, et terra glória tua. Hosánna in excélsis. Benedíctus † qui venit in nómine Dómini. Hosánna in excélsis.

Holy, Holy, Holy Lord God of Hosts. Heaven and earth are full of thy glory. Hosanna in the highest. Blessed † is he who comes in the name of the Lord. Hosanna in the highest.

CANON OF THE MASS
18. - Prayer for the Church

Te ígitur, clementíssime Pater, per Iesum Christum, Fílium tuum, Dóminum nostrum, súpplices rogámus ac pétimus, uti accépta hábeas, et benedícas, hæc † dona, hæc † múnera, hæc † sancta sacrifícia illibáta, in primis, quæ tibi offérimus pro Ecclésia tua sancta cathólica: quam pacificáre, custodíre, adunáre, et régere dignéris toto orbe terrárum: una cum fámulo tuo Papa nostro *"N."*, et Antístite nostro *"N."*, et ómnibus orthodóxis, atque cathólicæ et apostólicæ fídei cultóribus.

To thee, most merciful Father, we make our humble prayer, asking through Jesus Christ thy Son, our Lord, that thou wouldst receive and bless, these † gifts, these † presents, these † holy, spotless offerings. We offer them to thee first and foremost for thy holy catholic Church: be pleased, to give her peace, to protect, gather into one, and govern her, throughout the whole world. We offer them too for thy servant *"N."*, our Pope and for *"N."*, our Bishop and for all those who, faithful to the true teaching, are guardians of the catholic and apostolic faith.

19. - The commemoration of the living

eménto, Dómine, famulórum, famularúmque tuarum *("N." et "N.")...*

emember, Lord, thy servants, men and women *("N." and "N.")...*

After a brief pause praying for the living, he continues saying:

...et ómnium circumstántium, quorum tibi fides cógnita est et nota devótio, pro quibus tibi offérimus: vel qui tibi ófferunt hoc sacrifícium laudis, pro se suísque ómnibus: pro redemptióne animárum suárum, pro spe salútis et incolumitátis suæ: tibíque reddunt vota sua ætérno Deo, vivo et vero.

...and all those here around us: thou knowest their faith and proven loyalty. For them we offer thee this sacrifice of praise, or they offer it to thee for themselves, for all their own: to obtain redemption of their souls, the salvation they hope for and freedom from all danger: and they make their prayers to thee, the eternal, living and true God.

20. - The commemoration of the Saints

On some Holy Days this prayer and the next one (21) are different

ommunicántes, et memóriam venerántes, in primis gloriósæ semper Vírginis Maríæ, Genitrícis Dei et Dómini nostri Iesu Christi: sed et beáti Ioseph, eiúsdem Vírginis Sponsi, et beatórum Apos-

nited in one communion, we venerate before all others the memory of the glorious ever-virgin Mary, Mother of God, our Lord Jesus Christ: and the memory too of thy blessed Apos-

tolórum ac Mártyrum tuórum, Petri et Páuli, Andréæ, Iacóbi, Ioánnis, Thómæ, Iacóbi, Philíppi, Bartholomǽi, Matthǽi, Simónis, et Thaddǽi: Lini, Cleti, Cleméntis, Xysti, Cornélii, Cypriáni, Lauréntii, Chrisógoni, Ioánnis et Páuli, Cosmæ et Damiáni: et ómnium Sanctórum tuórum; quorum méritis precibúsque concédas, ut in ómnibus protectiónis tuæ muniámur auxilio. Per eúndem Christum Dóminum nostrum. Amen.

tles and Martyrs, Peter and Paul, Andrew, James, John, Thomas, James, Philip, Bartholomew, Matthew, Simon and Thaddeus, Linus, Cletus, Clement, Xystus, Cornelius, Cyprian, Laurence, Chrysogonus, John and Paul, Cosmas and Damian, and of all thy Saints. Through their merits and prayers, defend us in all circumstances by thine aid and protection. Through the same Christ our Lord. Amen.

21. - Jesus Christ, our Victim

Hanc ígitur oblatiónem servitútis nostræ, sed et cunctæ famíliæ tuæ, quǽsumus, Dómine, ut placátus accípias: diésque nostros in tua pace dispónas, atque ab ætérna damnatióne nos éripi, et in electórum tuórum iúbeas grege numerári. Per Christum Dóminum nostrum. Amen.

Be pleased then, Lord, to accept this offering from us thy servants and from thy whole family too; let it be thy will to dispose all our days in thy peace and to snatch us from eternal damnation and count us among the number of your chosen ones. Through Christ our Lord. Amen.

uam oblatiónem tu, Deus, in ómnibus, quǽsumus, benedíctam †, adscríptam †, ratam †, rationábilem, acceptabilémque fácere dignéris: ut nobis Corpus † et Sánguis † fiat dilectíssimi Fílii tui Dómini nostri Iesu Christi.

ay it seem fitting to thee, 0 God, to make this offering in every way, a blessed † offering, an acceptable † offering, an approved † offering, perfect and pleasing to thee: so that it may become for us, the Body † and Blood † of thy well-beloved Son, our Lord Jesus Christ.

22. - Consecration and elevation of the Host

The most solemn moment of the Mass has arrived. The Sacrifice that is offered on the altar is the same that was offered on Calvary: it is the same Priest and the same Victim. The bread is changed into the Body of Jesus Christ and the wine into his Blood. In a bloodless way the Blood of Jesus is separated from his sacred Body

ui prídie quam paterétur, accépit panem in sanctas ac venerábiles manus suas, et elevátis óculis in cælum ad te Deum Patrem suum omnipoténtem, tibi grátias agens, bene†díxit, fregit, dedítque discípulis suis, dicens: Accípite, et manducáte ex hoc omnes:

HOC EST ENIM CORPUS MEUM.

e it was who on the eve of his Passion, took bread in his holy and adorable hands, and looking up to heaven to thee, God, his almighty Father, giving thanks to thee, he † blessed the bread, broke it, and gave it to his disciples, saying: Take and eat of this, all of you.

FOR THIS IS MY BODY.

23. - Consecration and elevation of the Chalice

Símili modo póstquam cenátum est, accípiens et hunc præclárum Cálicem in sanctas ac venerábiles manus suas: item tibi grátias agens, bene†díxit, dedítque discípulis suis, dicens: Accípite, et bíbite ex eo omnes:

In like manner after the Supper, he took this noble Chalice in his holy and adorable hands: and giving thanks to thee, he blessed † it and gave it to his disciples, saying: Take and drink of this, all of you.

HIC EST ENIM CALIX SÁNGUINIS MEI, NOVI ET ÆTÉRNI TESTAMÉNTI: MYSTÉRIUM FÍDEI: QUI PRO VOBIS ET PRO MULTIS EFFUNDÉTUR IN REMISSIÓNEM PECCATÓRUM.

FOR THIS IS THE CHALICE OF MY BLOOD OF THE NEW AND ETERNAL TESTAMENT: THE MYSTERY OF THE FAITH: WHICH SHALL BE SHED FOR YOU AND FOR MANY FOR THE FORGIVENESS OF SINS.

Hæc quotiescúmque fecéritis, in mei memóriam faciétis.

As often as you shall do this, you shall do it in memory of me.

What is now on the altar is no longer bread or wine, but the true Body and Blood of Jesus Christ, alive and glorious

- 27 -

24. - Commemoration of the Passion, Resurrection and Ascension of the Lord

nde et mémores, Dómine, nos servi tui, sed et plebs tua sancta, eiúsdem Christi Fílii tui, Dómini nostri, tam beátæ passiónis, nec non et ab ínferis resurrectiónis, sed et in cælos gloriósæ ascensiónis: offérimus præcláræ maiestáti tuæ de tuis donis ac datis, hóstiam † puram, hóstiam † sanctam, hóstiam † inmaculatam, Panem † sanctum vitæ ætérnæ, et Cálicem † salútis perpétuæ.

or that reason, Lord, in memory of the blessed Passion of the same Christ, thy Son, our Lord, of his resurrection from the place of the dead, and of his ascension into the glory of heaven, we thy servants, together with thy holy people, present thy glorious majesty with this offering, taken from thine own good gifts, the perfect † victim, the holy † victim, the unblemished † victim, the holy † Bread of eternal life, and the Chalice † of eternal salvation.

25. - Recommendation of the Sacrifice

upra quæ propítio ac seréno vultu respícere dignéris: et accépta habére, sícuti accépta habére dignátus es múnera púeri tui iusti Abel, et sacrifícium Patriárchæ nostri Abrahæ: et quod tibi óbtulit summus sacérdos tuus Melchísedech, sanctum sacrifícium, immaculátam hóstiam.

urn thy face, in favour and kindliness, to these our offerings. Accept them as thou wert pleased to accept the gifts of thy servant Abel the Just, and the sacrifice of Abraham, our Father in faith, and that which thy high priest Melchizedek offered thee, a holy offering, a victim without blemish.

úpplices te rogámus, omnípotens Deus: iube hæc perférri per manus sancti Angeli tui in sublíme altáre tuum, in conspéctu divínæ maiestátis tuæ: ut quoquot ex hac altáris participatióne sacrosánctum Fílii tui, Cor✝pus, et Sán✝guinem sumpsérimus, omni benedictióne cælésti ✝ et grátia repleámur.
Per eúndem Christum Dóminum nostrum. Amen.

e humbly beg of thee, almighty God, have thy holy angel bear these gifts in his hands to thine altar on high, into the presence of thy divine majesty: so that when, in the communion of this altar, we shall receive the infinitely holy, ✝ Body and ✝ Blood of thy Son, we may all be filled with every blessing and grace from heaven.
Through the same Christ our Lord. Amen.

26. - Commemoration of the dead

We pray now for the dead. The souls in Purgatory are relieved during the Sacrifice offered for their intention due to the Communion of Saints. The priest reads the following words, optionally mentioning the name of the deceased ("N." and "N.")

eménto étiam, Dómine, famulórum famularúmque tuárum (*"N." et "N."*), qui nos præcessérunt cum signo fídei, et dórmiunt in somno pacis.

emember also, Lord, thy servants, (*"N." and "N."*), who have gone before us marked with the sign of the faith, and rest in the sleep of peace.

After a brief pause praying for the dead, he continues saying:

Ipsis, Dómine, et ómnibus in Christo quiescéntibus, locum refrigérii, lucis et pacis, ut indúlgeas, deprecámur. Per eúndem Christum Dóminum nostrum. Amen.

To those, Lord, and to all who take their rest in Christ, grant, we beg thee, the place of consolation, of light, and of peace. Through the same Christ our Lord. Amen.

27. - Prayer for us, sinners

The Church Militant and the Church Triumphant
are united to the Church Suffering

 obis quoque peccatóribus,...

 o us also, who are sinners,...

...fámulis tuis, de multitúdine miseratiónum tuárum sperántibus, partem áliquam et societátem donáre dignéris, cum tuis sanctis Apóstolis et Martýribus: cum Ioánne, Stéphano, Matthía, Bárnaba, Ignátio, Alexándro, Marcellíno, Petro, Felicitáte, Perpétua, Agatha, Lúcia, Agnéte, Cæcília, Anastásia, et ómnibus Sanctis tuis: intra quorum nos consórtium, non æstimátor mériti, sed véniæ, quǽsumus, largítor admítte. Per Christum Dóminum nostrum.

…thy servants, trusting in thine infinite mercy, grant of thy goodness a place in the fellowship of thy holy Apostles and Martyrs: with John, Stephen, Matthias, Barnabas, Ignatius, Alexander, Marcellinus, Peter, Felicity, Perpetua, Agatha, Lucy, Agnes, Cecilia, Anastasia, and with all thy Saints. Admit us to their company, we beg thee, not weighing what we deserve but generously pardoning us. Through Christ our Lord.

28. - End of the "Canon" and minor elevation

Per quem hæc ómnia, Dómine, semper bona creas, sanctí†ficas, viví†ficas, bene†dícis, et præstas nobis.

Through him, Lord, thou dost ever create, and make † holy, infuse † with life and bless † all these good things, thy gifts to us.

Per ipsum † , et cum ipso † , et in ipso † , est tibi Deo Patri † omnipoténti, in unitáte Spíritus † Sancti, omnis honor, et glória...

Through † him, and with † him, and in † him, be given to thee God, Father † Almighty, in the unity of the Holy † Spirit, all honour and all glory...

C) COMMUNION
29. - First Preparatory Prayer for Communion

...Per ómnia sǽcula sæculórum.

...World without end.

Amen.

Amen.

Orémus.

Let us pray.

Præcéptis salutáribus móniti, et divina institutióne formáti, audémus dícere:

Instructed by our Saviour's commands and trained by God's teaching we dare to say:

- 31 -

ater noster, qui es in cælis: sanctificétur nomen tuum; advéniat regnum tuum: fiat volúntas tua sicut in cælo et in terra. Panem nostrum quotidiánum da nobis hódie: et dimítte nobis débita nostra, sicut et nos dimíttimus debitóribus nostris. Et ne nos indúcas in tentatiónem.

Sed líbera nos a malo.

Amen.

íbera nos, quǽsumus, Dómine, ab ómnibus malis, prætéritis, præséntibus et futúris: et intercedénte beáta et gloriósa semper Vírgine Dei Genitríce María, cum beátis Apóstolis tuis Petro et Páulo, atque Andréa, et ómnibus Sanctis, † da propítius pacem in diébus nostris: ut, ope misericórdiæ tuæ adiúti, et a peccáto simus semper líberi, et ab omni perturbatióne secúri.

ur Father, who art in heaven, hallowed be thy name, thy kingdom come, thy will be done on earth as it is in heaven; give us this day our daily bread, and forgive us our trespasses as we forgive them that trespass against us, and lead us not into temptation:

But deliver us from evil.

Amen.

eliver us, Lord, we beg thee, from all evils past, present and future; and through the intercession of the blessed and glorious ever virgin Mary, Mother of God, and of the blessed Apostles Peter and Paul and Andrew, and of all the Saints, grant † peace in our days: so that helped by the workings of thy mercy we may be always free from sin and safe from all distress.

30. - Fraction of the Host

Per eúndem Dóminum nostrum Iesum Christum, Fílium tuum. Qui tecum vivit et regnat in unitáte Spíritus Sancti Deus,...

Through the same Jesus Christ our Lord, thy Son, who is God, living and reigning with thee in the unity of the Holy Spirit, God...

...per ómnia sæcula sæculórum.

...world without end.

Amen.

Amen.

ax † Dómini sit † semper vobís-†cum.

he peace of the † Lord be † always with † you.

Et cum spíritu tuo.

And with you also.

The Priest drops the particle of the Host into the Chalice

æc commíxtio et consecrátio Córporis et Sánguinis Dómini nostri Iesu Christi, fiat accipiéntibus nobis in vitam ætérnam. Amen.

ay this sacramental mingling of the Body and of the Blood of our Lord Jesus Christ, which we are about to receive, bring us eternal life. Amen.

31. - Second Preparatory Prayer for Communion: "Agnus Dei"

Agnus Dei, qui tollis peccáta mundi, miserére nobis.

Lamb of God, who takest away the sins of the world, have mercy on us.

Agnus Dei, qui tollis peccáta mundi, miserére nobis.

Lamb of God, who takest away the sins of the world, have mercy on us.

Agnus Dei, qui tollis peccáta mundi, dona nobis pacem.

Lamb of God, who takest away the sins of the world, give us peace.

32. - Prayer for peace

Dómine Iesu Christe, qui dixísti Apóstolis tuis: Pacem relínquo vobis, pacem meam do vobis: ne respícias peccáta mea, sed fidem Ecclésiæ tuæ: eámque secúndum voluntátem tuam pacificáre et coadunáre dignéris: Qui vivis et regnas Deus, per ómnia sæcula sæculórum. Amen.

Lord Jesus Christ, who hast said to thine Apostles: I leave you with peace, it is my peace I give you: turn not thy gaze upon my sins but upon the faith of thy Church, and according to thy will, grant her that peace and gather her together in unity: who livest and reignest God, world without end. Amen.

33. - Last Preparatory Prayers for Communion

ómine Iesu Christe, Fili Dei vivi, qui ex voluntáte Patris, cooperánte Spíritu Sancto, per mortem tuam mundum vivificásti: líbera me per hoc sacrosánctum Corpus et Sánguinem tuum ab ómnibus iniquitátibus meis, et univérsis malis: et fac me tuis semper inhærére mandátis, et a te numquam separári permíttas: Qui cum eódem Deo Patre et Spiritu Sancto vivis et regnas Deus in sæcula sæculórum. Amen.

Lord Jesus Christ, Son of the living God, who, in fulfillment of the Father's will, in a common work with the Holy Spirit, hast by thy death brought life to the world, deliver me by this thine infinitely holy Body and Blood from all my sins and from every evil. Make me always cleave to thy commandments and never let me become separated from thee: who art God, living and reigning with God the Father and the Holy Spirit, world without end. Amen.

ercéptio Córporis tui, Dómine Iesu Christe, quod ego indígnus súmere præsúmo, non mihi provéniat in iudícium et condemnatiónem: sed pro tua pietáte prosit mihi ad tutaméntum mentis et córporis, et ad medélam percipiéndam: Qui vivis et regnas cum Deo Patre in unitáte Spíritus Sancti Deus, per ómnia sæcula sæculórum. Amen.

Unworthy as I am, Lord Jesus Christ, I dare to receive thy Body; do not let that bring down upon me thy judgement and condemnation; through thy loving kindness let it be a safeguard and a healing remedy for my soul and body: who with God the Father in the unity of the Holy Spirit livest and reignest, God for ever and ever. Amen.

34. - Communion of the Celebrant

 anem cæléstem accípiam, et nomen Dómini invocábo.

 will take the Bread of heaven and I will call upon the name of the Lord.

 ómine, non sum dignus…

ord, I am not worthy,…

…ut intres sub tectum meum: sed tantum dic verbo, et sanábitur ánima mea.

…that thou shouldst enter under my roof; but say only the word and my soul shall be healed.

Dómine, non sum dignus… Lord, I am not worthy,…

…ut intres sub tectum meum: sed tantum dic verbo, et sanábitur ánima mea.

…that thou shouldst enter under my roof; but say only the word and my soul shall be healed.

Dómine, non sum dignus… Lord, I am not worthy,…

…ut intres sub tectum meum: sed tantum dic verbo, et sanábitur ánima mea.

…that thou shouldst enter under my roof; but say only the word and my soul shall be healed.

Corpus Dómini nostri † Iesu Christi custódiat ánimam meam in vitam ætérnam. Amen.

The Body of our Lord † Jesus Christ be my soul's protection for life eternal. Amen.

And receives Communion under the species of bread.
While collecting the particles that have been detached from the large
Host, he prepares to consume the Chalice, saying:

Quid retríbuam Dómino pro ómnibus quæ retríbuit mihi? Cálicem salutáris accípiam, et nomen Dómini invocábo. Láudans invocábo Dóminum, et ab inimícis meis salvus ero.

What shall I give to God in return for all his gifts to me? I will take the Chalice of salvation and I will call upon the name of the Lord. I will praise the Lord as I call upon him, and I shall be safe from my enemies.

Sanguis Dómini nostri † Iesu Christi custódiat ánimam meam in vitam ætérnam. Amen.

May the Blood of our Lord † Jesus Christ be my soul's protection for life eternal. Amen.

And receives Communion under the species of wine

35. - Communion of the faithful

Showing the sacred Host to the faithful, he says:

Ecce Agnus Dei, ecce qui tollit peccáta mundi.

Behold the Lamb of God, behold him who takest away the sins of the world.

Dómine, non sum dignus ut intres sub tectum meum: sed tantum dic verbo et sanábitur ánima mea.

Lord, I am not worthy, that thou shouldst enter under my roof; but say only the word and my soul shall be healed.

Dómine, non sum dignus ut intres sub tectum meum: sed tantum dic verbo et sanábitur ánima mea.

Lord, I am not worthy, that thou shouldst enter under my roof; but say only the Word and my soul shall be healed.

Dómine, non sum dignus ut intres sub tectum meum: sed tantum dic verbo et sanábitur ánima mea.

Lord, I am not worthy, that thou shouldst enter under my roof; but say only the Word and my soul shall be healed.

Those who are going to receive Communion must do so in their mouth and on their knees (unless some health problem prevents it). In administering Communion, the Priest says each time:

Corpus Dómini nostri Iesu † Christi custódiat ánimam tuam in vitam ætérnam. Amen.

The Body of our Lord Jesus † Christ preserve thy soul unto life everlasting. Amen.

Amen is not answered.
The communicant goes back to his place for thanksgiving

36. - Thanksgiving

Meanwhile, the chalice is purified with wine and water.

Quod ore súmpsimus, Dómine, pura mente capiámus: et de múnere temporáli fiat nobis remédium sempitérnum.

What our mouths have eaten, Lord, may our souls receive with purity and may the gift we receive in this life be for us a remedy for life eternal.

Corpus tuum, Dómine, quod sumpsi, et Sanguis, quem potávi, adhǽreat viscéribus meis: et præsta, ut in me non remáneat scélerum mácula, quem pura et sancta refecérunt Sacraménta: Qui vivis et regnas in sǽcula sæculórum. Amen.

May thy Body which I have eaten, Lord, and thy Blood which I have drunk, cleave to my innermost being; and grant that nothing of sin's defilement may remain in me, now that I have been renewed by this Sacrament so pure and holy: who livest and reignest world without end. Amen.

37. - Communion and Postcommunion

The last two proper prayers for each day. First the antiphon called "Communion" and after kissing the altar, he turns to the people and says:

Dóminus vobíscum.

The Lord be with you.

Et cum spíritu tuo.

And with you also.

Orémus.

Let us pray.

And he recites the "Postcommunion" prayer,
which can be more than one. The response is:

Amen.   Amen.

And again he kisses the altar and says:

Dóminus vobíscum.   The Lord be with you.

Et cum spíritu tuo.   And with your spirit.

38. - Dismissal

Ite, missa est.   Go, the Mass is ended.

Deo grátias.   Thanks be to God.

39. - Blessing

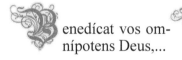 láceat tibi, sancta Trinitas, obsé-quium servitútis meæ: et præsta; ut sacrifícium, quod óculis tuæ maiestátis indígnus óbtuli, tibi sit acceptábile, mihíque et ómnibus, pro quibus illud óbtuli, sit, te miseránte, propitiábile. Per Christum Dóminum nostrum. Amen.

ay the homage of my service, 0 holy Trinity, be pleasing to thee; and grant that the sacrifice, which I, though unworthy, have offered in the sight of thy majesty, may be acceptable to thee, and through thy mercy bring forgiveness to me and all for whom I have offered it. Through Christ our Lord. Amen.

enedícat vos omnípotens Deus,...   ay Almighty God bless you:...

And turning to the faithful, he blesses them saying:

✝ ...Pater, † et Fílius, et Spíritus Sanctus.

...the Father, the Son, † and the Holy Spirit.

Amen.

Amen.

40. - Last Gospel and end of Mass

Dóminus vobíscum.

The Lord be with you.

Et cum spíritu tuo.

And with your spirit.

✛ Inítium sancti † Evangélii † secúndum † Ioánnem.

The beginning of the holy † Gospel † according to † John.

Glória tibi, Dómine.

Glory to thee, 0 Lord.

In princípio erat Verbum, et Verbum erat apud Deum, et Deus erat Verbum. Hoc erat in princípio apud Deum. Omnia per ipsum facta sunt: et sine ipso factum est nihil, quod factum est: in ipso vita erat, et vita erat lux hóminum: et lux in ténebris lucet, et ténebræ eam non comprehendérunt. Fuit homo missus a Deo, cui nomen erat Ioánnes. Hic venit in testimónium, ut testimónium

In the beginning was the Word, and the Word was with God, and the Word was God. He was in the beginning with God. All things were made through him, and without him was made nothing that was made. In him was life, and life was the light of men, and the light shines in the darkness, and the darkness did not comprehend it. A man came, sent from God, whose name was John. He came as a witness, to give testimony to the light, that

perhibéret de lúmine, ut omnes créderent per illum. Non erat ille lux, sed ut testimónium perhibéret de lúmine. Erat lux vera, quæ illúminat omnem hóminem veniéntem in hunc mundum. In mundo erat, et mundus per ipsum factus est, et mundus eum non cognóvit. In propria venit, et sui eum non recepérunt. Quotquot autem recepérunt eum, dedit eis potestátem fílios Dei fíeri, his, qui crédunt in nómine eius: qui non ex sanguínibus, neque ex voluntáte carnis, neque ex voluntáte viri, sed ex Deo nati sunt...

...ET VERBUM CARO FACTUM EST,...

...et habitávit in nobis: et vídimus glóriam eius, glóriam quasi Unigéniti a Patre, plenum grátiæ et veritátis.

Deo grátias.

all might believe through him. He was not the light, but was to give testimony to the light. The Word was the true Light, which enlightens every man who comes into the world. He was in the world, and the world was made through him, and the world did not recognise him. He came to his own, and his own did not receive him, but to all who did receive him, and who believe in his name, to these he gave power to become children of God born not of blood, nor by the will of flesh, nor by the will of man, but of God...

...AND THE WORD BECAME FLESH,...

...and dwelt among us; and we saw his glory, the glory of the only-begotten of the Father, full of grace and truth.

Thanks be to God.

Holy Mass has ended

Thanksgiving after Mass

The Sacred Liturgy exhorts and desires that everyone who, receiving communion, has participated in the divine delicacy, render due thanks to God for it. It indicates to the priest and the faithful, within the Mass itself, a minimum of thanksgiving; but it also provides, to continue it, other indulgent prayers, and exhorts everyone to make of the Christian life an uninterrupted hymn of gratitude. And Pope Pius XII adds: "It is very convenient that, after having received Communion and finished the public rites, the communicant is gathered, and intimately united with the Divine Master, is entertained with Him in a most sweet and healthy conversation, during the whole time allowed by circumstances."

What is the Mass?

The Holy Mass is the Sacrifice of the New Law, in which Jesus Christ offers himself and sacrifices himself for the whole Church under the species of bread and wine, through the ministry of the Priest, to recognize the supreme dominion of God and to apply to us the satisfactions and merits of his Passion. The Holy Mass is the same and unique Sacrifice of Christ on the Cross.

What are the ends of the Mass?

There are four: the latreutic, to give God the supreme cult of adoration; the Eucharistic, to give thanks to God for his immense benefits; the impetratory, to ask God for spiritual and temporal goods; and the expiatory, to satisfy God for the sins and penalties deserved by them, both of the dead and of the living. When one attends Mass, then, it is Jesus Christ himself who acts: he is the one who adores his Father for us. He is the one who thanks Him for his benefits, He is the one who offers thanks, He is the one who appeases Him. Hence, Mass is the best adoration, the best thanksgiving, the best impetratory prayer, and the best act of atonement. No practice of piety can equal the Mass, and no act of religion, public or private, can be more pleasing to God and useful to man; hence it must be the devotion par excellence of the Christian.

CPSIA information can be obtained
at www.ICGtesting.com
Printed in the USA
BVHW022155120922
646876BV00021B/194

9 781732 288522